DISCARDED

DATE DUE		
OCT 26 1990	OCT 1 4 2004	
JAN		
MAY 5 1998	JAN 5 '09	
SEP 1 5 1998		
	MAR 31 1998	
JA 17 '95		
MY 25 '95	SEP 21 1999	
	APR 2 5 2000	
OC 16 '95	MY 19 '00	
DE 21 '95	MY 25 '00	
APR 28 1998		
NOV 04 1998	AG 30 '01	

D1223273

HUMPBACK WHALE

CONTENTS

© Aladdin Books Ltd 1989

*First published in
the United States in 1990 by*
Gloucester Press
387 Park Avenue South
New York NY10016

Design Rob Hillier, Andy Wilkinson
Editor Fiona Robertson
Photo Research Cecilia Weston-Baker
Illustrations Ron Hayward Associates

Printed in Belgium

Library of Congress Cataloging-in-Publication Data

Bright, Michael
    Humpback whale/Michael Bright
       p. cm -- (Project Wildlife)
    Summary: Describes the characteristics of humpback whales,
their feeding habits, migration routes and vulnerability to hunters.
Also discusses efforts, by such groups as Greenpeace, to preserve
them as a species.
    ISBN 0-531-17216-3
    1. Humpback whale--Juvenile literature. [1. Humpback whale. 2.
Whales.] I. Title. II Series.
QL737. C424B75 1990
599.5'1--dc20
                            89-28779 CIP AC

PROJECT WILDLIFE

HUMPBACK WHALE

Michael Bright

Gloucester Press
New York : London : Toronto : Sydney

Introduction

The huge humpback is the most acrobatic of the great whales.

The humpback whale is probably the most familiar of the giant baleen whales. It was also once the most endangered. The species evolved around 10 million years ago and, because of its ability to adapt to change, continued to thrive.

But what nature created all that time ago, the whale fishery nearly destroyed in just a few years. Only action in the 1960s to ban the commercial hunting of the humpback saved it from extinction. Today, although its numbers are still low, this gentle giant can be found in all the oceans of the world. It is most famous for its enchanting but melancholy song, a sound that has become the symbolic voice for all the whales.

In 1986, a moratorium, or agreed ban, on commercial whaling was passed to protect the species. It is set to last until 1990. What will happen at the end of the moratorium is uncertain.

Humpback whale distribution

Humpback whales are seen in coastal waters all over the world. In the summer they feed in polar regions and in winter they breed in the tropics, with one exception — those in the Arabian Sea appear to stay the whole year round. In the rest of the world, there are three distinct populations that rarely meet. There are humpbacks in the north Atlantic, north Pacific, and those scattered throughout the southern hemisphere. Those in the north do not cross the equator to visit those in the south. The northern winter is the southern summer so the whales' breeding cycles are six months out of step. The major populations are subdivided into smaller stocks that tend to visit the same breeding or feeding sites. Some stocks intermingle. Those that feed in summer near the Alaskan coast, for example, are seen either off the Mexican coast or in Hawaiian waters during the winter.

▽ Individual whales can be identified by the shape and color of their tail fluke.

Recognizing individuals makes counting whales easier and more accurate.

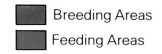

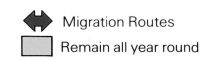

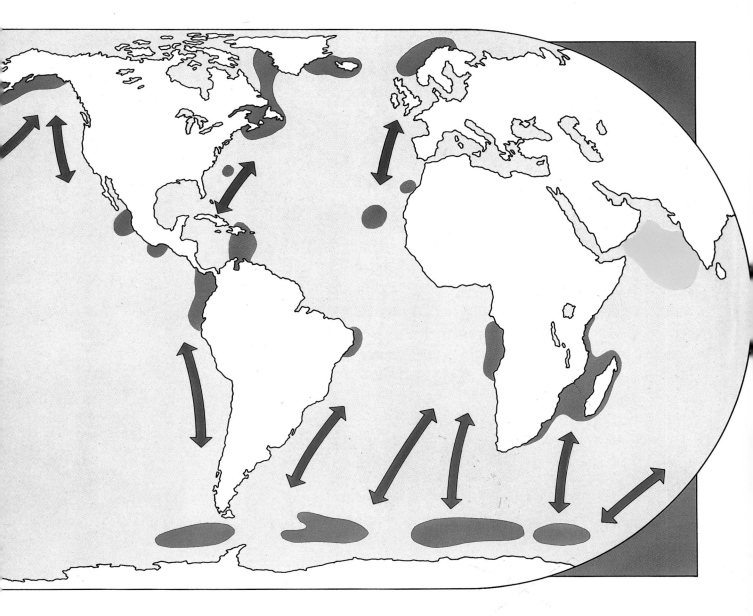

△ Humpback whales go on long migrations. In the map above, the migration routes link courtship and calving sites in the warm tropical waters with the fish and krill rich cold waters of polar regions. The regularity of the migrations meant that hunters simply waited at strategic points along the route and attacked the whales as they passed by.

Before the hunting, there were estimated to be around 100-150,000 humpback whales in the world. Today, little more than 10,000 remain. The largest stock is found in the western Atlantic where over 5,000 whales live. About 1,000 are found in the north Pacific, and 3,700 in the southern hemisphere. The breeding and feeding areas are not all ancient sites that the whales have been visiting for thousands of years. The Hawaiian breeding site, for example, has only been in use for about 140 years.

Whale hunting

The first whalers did not venture far from land and so would probably have caught coastal-living species like the humpback. Between 4,000-2,000 BC, whaling was taking place on the coasts off Norway and Alaska. During the 11th century, the Basques had an extensive whaling industry, which concentrated mainly upon right whales. By 1800 they had effectively fished all such whales out of the eastern Atlantic. It was the first warning of the dangers of overfishing.

But the impact of whaling was not a serious threat to whales worldwide until humpbacks, along with all the other species of baleen whales, were exploited commercially in the 19th century.

For over a hundred years, whales were slaughtered with little regard for their long-term survival. They were caught, chopped up and melted down for their oil and meat.

△ Humpback baleen (the horny bristles in a whale's mouth with which it strains its food) was considered ideal for stiffening in women's corsets. Whale oil was used to make soap.

At first, whales were caught to provide food and oil for the community. In several parts of the world, that tradition continues today. This "aboriginal" whaling is exempt from the present worldwide ban on whaling.

Humpbacks are still hunted occasionally from small boats at Bequia in the West Indies, in the Cape Verde Islands in the eastern Atlantic and along the Greenland coast. There is concern that the whales taken by the Greenland villagers are from a limited stock and even this small-scale hunting could endanger the population.

Several of the large whaling nations have tried to "beat" the moratorium by claiming that their whaling industry is traditional. Another way to get around the ban is to claim that whales are caught for scientific research.

Eskimo whalers pursued whales from large canoes, and used harpoons tipped with bone or slate. A sealskin float was attached to a harpooned whale with lances. The whale eventually died of its wounds and its position was marked by the buoy. It was towed ashore and cut up. Nothing was wasted. Blubber and meat were eaten, the sinews were used for rope, and the gut was dried and inflated to store oil.

▷ This Greenland eskimo is cutting up whale meat and drying it in the sun. This is one of the few areas left in the world where humpback whales are still killed. The hunt is traditional, but the boats and weapons are more likely to be modern.

◁ In ancient times, whalers went to sea in open boats and caught whales with hand-held harpoons. It was very dangerous as the whales often towed the boats until they were exhausted. Male humpbacks sometimes charged the whaling boats, causing them to cave in, and the crews to drown.

The slaughter continues

Whaling was very much a "boom-and-bust" industry. When whale stocks were exhausted in one area, whalers simply moved on and "fished out" another. In the Atlantic, first the Basques, and then the British, Dutch, Scandinavian, French, and German whalers slaughtered most of the whales in the Arctic and then moved on. American whalers took the majority of the whales in the western Atlantic before going south.

All the whaling nations, including Japan, Norway, the Soviet Union and Korea, ended up in the Southern Ocean. First they took the easily caught right and humpback whales. Then modern fleets, with faster boats and explosive harpoons, killed the blue whale (the largest whale), followed by the fin, the sei, and the minke (the smallest baleen whale).

At the end of the 19th century, Norwegian inventor Svend Foyn developed the explosive harpoon. It was fired into the whale's body where an explosive charge released four barbs that caught fast inside the whale. This ensured the harpoon did not pull out, and the whale towed the catcher boat for up to two hours until tired. When blood spurted from the whale's blowhole, the whalers knew that the whale would soon die.

◁ The invention of the explosive harpoon meant that whales could be caught more easily.

△ The photograph above shows the moment the heavy harpoon slams into the whale's body.

Modern whaling fleets consisted of a flotilla of small, fast catcher-boats which served either a shore station or a liner-sized factory ship. The dead whales were filled with compressed air to make them float and rounded up by a collecting boat. Then they were taken to the factory ship where they were sliced up and melted down.

A catcher boat could kill as many as 50 whales in a day. Earlier whaling crews did not kill so many whales at a time, except for those crews that caught humpbacks. Humpback whales were not rich in oil, but were easy to catch in large numbers because they gathered regularly at known feeding or breeding sites. Large female humpbacks with calves were easy targets. The whalers would harpoon the calf and then take the mother when she came to its rescue.

"It was a terrible, cruel death. It would have been impossible to continue whaling if the whales could only cry out or scream. I was very glad they couldn't."

A Shetland whaler who fished in the south Atlantic.

▽ At an Icelandic whaling station a whale carcass is taken apart. Iceland is one of the few nations that continues to catch whales for "scientific" purposes. Most of the meat is sold to Japan.

Destruction of the oceans

For centuries, the oceans have been used as a universal dumping ground. It was thought that pollutants would be diluted and dispersed in the sea and never seen again. How wrong we were!

First they are taken up by the plankton, which in turn are eaten by small fish or shrimps. These are engulfed in huge quantities by the giant whales. Each mouthful of food is also accompanied by the poisons concentrated in the tiny bodies. The whales, throughout their long lives, have been accumulating these substances, storing them in their blubber and in the liver.

Humpbacks are particularly vulnerable to marine pollution. They live in the coastal waters that are more likely to contain high concentrations of pollutants. Already, tissue analysis from dead humpbacks that have been washed ashore has shown high levels of PCBs and DDT, two substances that were once in widespread use, but are now banned or in limited use. Yet here they are today, returning once more to the surface in the bodies of whales — a legacy from the past.

The pesticide DDT, industrial chemicals known as PCBs, and heavy metals like mercury and lead, are the most feared of marine pollutants. At high levels they can prevent conception, cause birth defects, brain damage and death. In 1987, the deaths of 16 humpback whales was thought to be caused by coastal pollution.

▽ The 1989 oil spill off Alaska came from the tanker in the photograph below. The area affected not only contains the breeding sites of fur seals, but also the summer feeding grounds of humpback whales.

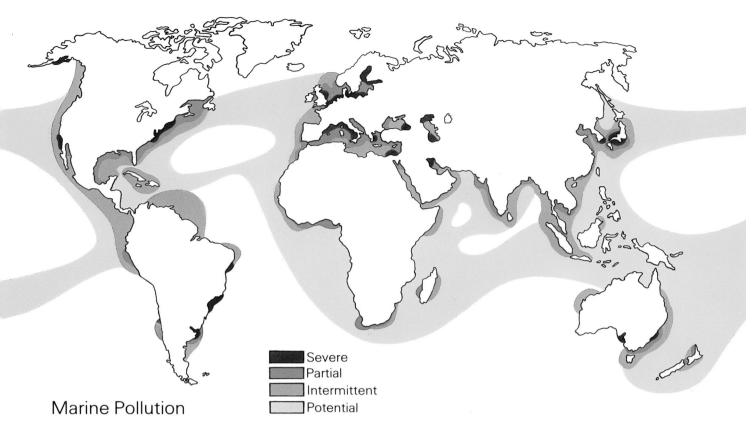

Severe
Partial
Intermittent
Potential

Marine Pollution

△ The areas of severe marine pollution marked on the map above, coincide with the migration routes of humpback whales (see map on pages 6-7). Twice each year, whales must pass through polluted seas.

The humpback whale is also vulnerable to human disturbance and noise pollution. Their mating grounds are in shallow waters, and whales might be disrupted by coastal recreational and commercial traffic. Humpbacks are particularly vocal animals and the noise from boat engines could interfere with whale communication.

△ This whale could have died and beached itself for a variety of reasons.

But, there is growing concern that whales are being poisoned by pollution.

Overfishing

Whales and people often compete for the same food resources. If fishermen catch too many fish or shrimps they can move on to another place and catch something else. The whales cannot. Deprived of their food, they either stop breeding, or at worst, starve. In some parts of the world there is a danger that this could happen.

Humpback whales in the northern hemisphere eat mostly small fish, like capelin. Those in the southern hemisphere exist on small shrimp-like krill. The krill are found in huge schools that can even be tracked by satellites in space. They are the mainstay of the Antarctic food chain, sustaining fish, squid, penguins, seals and whales. Unfortunately, the krill are also caught in enormous quantities by Japanese fishermen.

Humpbacks in the north-western Atlantic feed in the fish rich waters frequented by fishing fleets from all over the world. They not only have to deal with the competition for food, but must also watch out for unexpected hazards. On their migration north, humpbacks passing the Newfoundland coast are confronted with a maze of mile-long, invisible drift nets. Many whales are trapped and die in the nets.

▽ Krill are small ocean-dwelling crustaceans. They live on the surface and are scooped up by whales.

If frightened by a smaller predator, they can literally jump out of their skins and escape.

If the krill of the Southern Ocean is harvested and overfished, all life in the Antarctic region will suffer. Whales, in particular, need huge quantities of krill in order to survive. They not only have to feed for the summer, but must also put on enough fat to take them through a six-month fast during the winter breeding period.

With a food item that weighs only a fraction of an ounce, each whale must eat a lot of krill. A large whale needs to eat up to two tons of krill per day, just to stay alive. The polar regions are very rich in food and can sustain great quantities of life. But if man interferes with that natural balance by removing a large portion at the bottom of the food chain, there is no way of knowing what will happen to life in the Antarctic.

▽ Japan has very little land on which to grow crops and so is dependent on the sea for food to feed its very large population. Japanese fishing fleets scour the world's oceans for potential foods. Lately they have turned to the Southern Ocean and have been exploiting the krill. The schools are skimmed from the sea's surface in trawls. In the photograph below, a trawl is being hauled on board. The krill is deep frozen and shipped back to Japan, mostly for animal food, although some is used for human consumption.

Protection

The International Whaling Commission (IWC) is the organization responsible for the regulation of whaling. It was started in 1946 by the whaling nations, not to save the whale, but to ensure that enough whales were alive to be caught in the future. In 1972, the United Nations Conference on the Environment in Stockholm suggested the IWC change the emphasis from the whalers to the whale. In recent years, non-whaling nations have joined the IWC and have forced the whalers to consider a complete ban on all whaling.

In 1986, a five year temporary moratorium on commercial whaling was agreed, and in 1988 Japan was the last nation to stop hunting. The main whaling nations, like Japan, the Soviet Union, North Korea, Norway and Iceland, are however, reluctant to stop whaling. Some have continued under the pretense of "scientific" or "aboriginal" whaling, which the IWC is powerless to control, or ban.

△ The IWC, whose insignia can be seen above, has 41 member nations, but lacks the power to stop whaling.

▽ Today, the IWC is a forum in which views and scientific information are exchanged. Decisions are made by compromise and international trading. One nation's right to fish in foreign waters may, for example, depend on their killing fewer whales.

For centuries, the humpback whale has been overexploited. In 1937, the population in the Antarctic was declining and a minimum catch length of 35ft was set. In 1939, the situation got worse and a complete ban was imposed. In 1946, the IWC allowed a limited catch of humpbacks, which was further changed to restrict catching to just four days in the year. Humpbacks in the north Atlantic received total protection in 1956. In 1963, there was a complete ban on killing humpbacks in the southern hemisphere. In 1966, humpbacks all over the world were saved from commercial exploitation when a ban was imposed on catching Pacific humpbacks. In all areas, whaling was stopped just in time. Each population was close to extinction.

△ In April 1980, two Spanish "pirate" whaling ships which were catching whales illegally, were sunk in Vigo harbor by militant conservationists from the *Sea Shepherd*.

"Caring about whales is a mark of personal and societal maturity."

Victor Scheffer Marine mammal scientist and author of *The Year of the Whale*

Monitoring the agreement

During the years when commercial whaling was regulated and catch quotas were in force, observers from IWC countries would ride with whaling ships and monitor catches. But for those who wanted a ban on whaling altogether this was not enough. Unofficial "policing" was carried out by conservation groups. Greenpeace adopted a nonaggressive approach. By buzzing around whale-fishing fleets in small boats, they hoped to make it difficult for whalers to catch whales.

The crew of the *Sea Shepherd*, however, used tougher measures. Using terrorist style tactics, they rammed and blew up pirate whaling ships. Both groups, in their own way, drew world attention to the plight of whales.

The "Save the Whale" campaign led by conservationists cannot take all the credit for the present moratorium on commercial whaling. Before they had even formed their anti-whaling groups, dedicated whale scientists had already alerted the whaling nations to the rapid decline of whale stocks, and the political battle to save whales was well underway.

Dear Tesco.
DON'T BUY YOUR
FISH FROM A
BUTCHER.
GREENPEACE
ICELAND KILLS WHALES. DON'T BUY THEIR FISH.

△ Greenpeace produced this postcard to discourage a food supermarket chain from buying their fish from Iceland. In this way, economic pressure might be brought on Iceland to stop "scientific whaling," as Iceland depends on exports to other countries.

◁ Greenpeace crews in inflatable rubber boats attempt to put themselves between whale-catchers and whales to stop them firing their harpoons.

Despite the ban on commercial whaling, whales are still being killed, especially for "scientific" purposes. Japan, Norway and Iceland propose that one way to monitor whale stocks is to take representative samples, that is, to kill a certain number of whales. This "scientific whaling" is worrying, for previous estimates of whale stocks are now known to have been exaggerated. "Scientific whalers" could therefore be contributing to the extinction of a stock rather than conserving it as they claim.

In the Southern Ocean there are fewer blue whales than was thought. If a scientific kill had been based on the previous figures, it is likely the population would have been wiped out. Blue whales are not being taken, but others such as the fin and sei whale are. Are scientific whalers putting these whale stocks at risk?

△ Conservation groups hold rallies to ensure that whales are kept in the headlines.

They remind the world that the moratorium is temporary and that whales are still being killed.

Humpback research

Whale research has been aimed mainly at finding ways in which populations can be accurately assessed. With a creature that spends much of its time below the surface, it is difficult not to count the same whale twice and overestimate the numbers in each whale stock. A few scientists believe that a small sample of whales must be caught in order to obtain information about the size, distribution, age and reproductive potential of the stock.

Others disagree, and have developed different techniques which do not harm whales. The latest is called "genetic fingerprinting." A tiny sample is taken from the skin of a living whale. The information contained in the nucleus of each cell can identify the whale, and even tell us which whales were its parents.

△ A group of humpbacks allow a scientist to come close. The data he obtains will provide more insight into whale life.

"DNA fingerprinting can provide from a tiny scrap of skin all the information about stock assessment which 'scientific whalers' promise from entire whales."

**Roger Payne
President, Long Term
Research Institute.**

Scientists can identify individual humpback whales by the distinctive white marks, scratches and wounds on their tail flukes. By building up a photographic record of whales' tails, the local movements and long distance migrations of each whale can be monitored. Using this technique, scientists in the eastern Pacific discovered that whales feeding off Alaska in summer could choose to go either to California or to Hawaii to breed in the winter.

△ The humpback shown above has very distinct markings on its tail flukes. The striations, however, are the teeth marks of killer whales. No doubt this whale was once chased by a pod of killer whales when it was in its polar feeding grounds. The injuries have left permanent scars, which scientists can use to identify the whale.

Whale watching

Humpbacks and other whales have certainly captured the public imagination. Everyone would like to see and even touch a whale. As a coastal species, humpbacks are relatively easy to watch, and the new whale watching industry has been quick to exploit this novel form of tourism.

Humpbacks on migration are predictable, so tourist boats can almost guarantee seeing a whale. Interestingly, the same predictability that was the downfall of the humpback is now contributing to its recovery. In some parts of the world, skippers who once killed humpbacks are now guiding tourists and offering expert advice.

▽ The whale watching boat in the photograph below is very close to two adult humpback whales on their spring migration to northern feeding grounds. The watchers have a good view of the enormous pectoral fin that has been raised in the air. The skipper of the boat must be careful that he does not place his vessel in the path of the whales. He must also not come between a mother and her calf.

Whale watching boats often have whale scientists on board. They not only give expert commentary, but can also carry out scientific observations. In this way, the new industry can contribute to whale research.

Whale watching, however, could cause problems. Unregulated boat operations may interfere with the whales' everyday lives. This could be critical at certain times, such as during mating or feeding. Groups of harassed whales might move elsewhere and breeding sites could be abandoned. Where stocks are low, disturbance could be disastrous.

In the United States and Canada, there are guidelines for whale watching boats. A boat must not come closer than 100ft in the United States to a whale. If a whale approaches the boat, a skipper should "put the engine in neutral and not re-engage the props until the whale is seen at the surface, clear of the boat."

▽ There are many places where tourist whale watching boats intercept humpback whales on migration. The most popular is along the New England coast of the United States.

Sometimes humpbacks will approach boats and perform remarkable aquabatics to the delight and cheers of all the people on board. The best time to watch whales is during the spring.

The future

The humpback whale was saved just in time and the numbers in the three main populations are increasing again. But, with a slow rate of reproduction, it will take many years before stocks are at their former levels. Although humpbacks are safe from whalers for the present, there are other threats, such as accidental drowning in fishing nets, overfishing and the pollution of the oceans. The latter two are hidden dangers. Their effects will not be immediately obvious, and once spotted it could be too late.

Stocks of humpbacks are still quite low and a contagious disease, like the one that has been killing seals in the North Sea, could easily wipe them out. In addition, with increasing marine traffic, conflict could arise between the interests of man and those of whales.

One remedy is to create whale sanctuaries where whales can live, at least for part of the year, without harassment. A sanctuary already exists on the breeding grounds at Maui, Hawaii. Others are proposed for Silver Bank in the West Indies, Campbell Island in New Zealand, Tonga, eastern Australia and other humpback mating and calving sites. The humpback has survived and adapted to change for ten million years. With our help, it could continue to do so.

Humpback calves often [ride] on their mother's back, where they are safe from predators. They can be left or right "handed:" some p[refer] to swim over their moth[er's] right flipper and some ov[er] the left.

"Amiable, fondest of parents, content to play about the shores of the most beautiful beaches in the world, and immune from attack of man everywhere.... So that the joyous Humpback is practically free to enjoy his life, to eat and love and play in the vastest playground given by God."

Frank Bullen 19th century author and seaman

Whale fact file 1

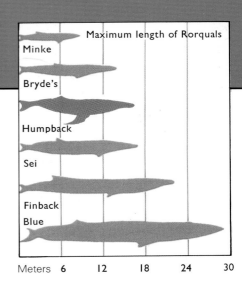

Humpback whales can grow to 50 feet in length and weigh up to 65 tons. They can live for up to 95 years. They are known as baleen whales because of the rows of stiff bristles, or baleen, in the mouth.

They are also grouped with the rorqual whales because of the pleated folds of skin along the throat.

Markings

Humpbacks are basically black above and on the flanks. The undersides are white. The flippers can be black above and white below, spotted, marbled, piebald or completely white. North Atlantic humpbacks have mostly white flippers. South Atlantic ones have black flippers. The tail flukes also vary from all black to those with white patterns. The head has rows of large knobs.

△ The humpback is distinguished from other rorquals by its gigantic pectoral fins, each with ten protruberances along the leading edge.

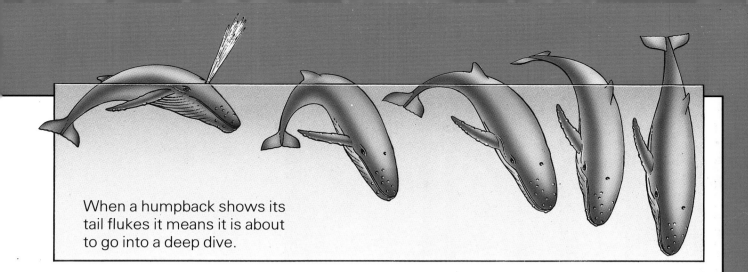

When a humpback shows its tail flukes it means it is about to go into a deep dive.

Swimming

The humpback is a graceful swimmer and an incredible underwater acrobat. The large flippers give this bulky creature amazing agility. Main propulsion is by the muscular tail.

On their long migrations, humpbacks swim along the surface, in pods of three to five whales. They move slowly at speeds of 6-12mph, breathing frequently at the surface. Occasionally they arch the back, show the tail fluke, and dive below.

Humpbacks often roll over in the water and wave a white knobby pectoral fin high in the air. At other times they raise their tail flukes high above the water and then bring them crashing down. This is known as tail-lobbing, and is thought to be one way whales can tell each other about their location in the sea. Some whales push their heads out of the water. This is called spy-hopping.

Humpbacks are well known for leaping clear of the water and crashing back down. It is called breaching, and is believed to be one way of dislodging parasites such as whale lice or barnacles, which attach themselves to these slow swimming creatures. Breaching might also be a means of communicating when conditions are bad.

Blowholes

A whale breathes each time it surfaces. Twin blowholes are on the top of the head. On surfacing, it must first clear the water in each blowhole. Then, before diving, it must take a breath and close the blowhole. The lungs are not large. It is not the amount of oxygen that allows it to stay underwater, but the way it stores and uses the oxygen in the blood and muscles.

Whale fact file 2

Food and feeding

The humpback whale is a filter feeder. This enormous animal feeds on tiny creatures, such as small fish or krill, which are skimmed from the sea's surface in large quantities. The whale opens its gigantic maw, or mouth, and takes in a mouthful of seawater. Then it closes its mouth, raises its tongue and squeezes the water out through the baleen bristles. Any food in the seawater soup is trapped and swallowed.

The most common method of feeding is known as lunge-feeding. The whale pushes across the surface of the water, scooping out the fish or krill which live there as it moves along. Sometimes a group of whales will swim in a line, herding the prey ahead of them.

Cooperation in humpback feeding is, however, limited. When whales come to the surface they will often push and shove to get to the greatest concentrations of prey.

One lone humpback was seen to feed in a most peculiar way. It came to the surface, lying vertically in the water, and then sank directly down. As it descended, a turbulent area of water, like the water leaving a bathtub, appeared above the mouth. The small fish were caught in the whirlpool and swept into the whale's mouth.

Bubble-net feeding

An unusual method of feeding is carried out by whales in Alaskan waters. It is called bubble-net feeding. A whale dives below a school of small fish and begins to blow bubbles. It circles under the school so that a cylinder of bubbles floats to the surface. The bubbles surround the fish and reflections of light on the surface confuse the fish, frightening them into the center of the cylinder. Then, without warning, the whale swims rapidly up through the center of the cylinder with its mouth wide open, gathering up all the fish that have been trapped there. Pleats under the mouth allow the throat to expand, and the whale takes a huge gulp.

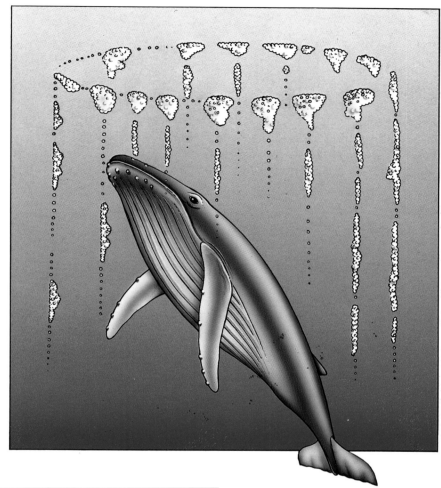

Barnacles

The humpback's skin is often covered with barnacles. There are three main types. One type favors the throat pleats and the belly. Another type lives on the tail, the lips and the leading edge of the flippers. The third barnacle does not attach itself directly to the whale, but lives on the other barnacles. Whales in the southeastern Atlantic often go into fresh water in order to dislodge their passengers.

Whale fact file 3

Singing

Humpback whales are very vocal animals. When in their feeding grounds they continually grunt and burp. But, in the breeding grounds they sing the most beautiful, yet melancholy, songs.

It is thought that the males do the singing. Whether the song tells other males to stay clear or invites females to come nearer is not clear. The breeding area is thought to resemble a lek, or gathering. The dominant males are at the center, in the best position to impress the females that come to visit the lek. When a female passes by, the following series of events might take place:

A cow humpback, accompanied by the calf she gave birth to the previous year, passes close to a singing male. The male stops singing and approaches the cow and calf (1). He takes up position alongside the pair, and the three swim along together (2). Sometimes the cow and bull disappear below, leaving the calf at the surface (3). This is likely to be the time when mating occurs. When the cow and bull return (4) they might be joined by other bulls (5). They bump and fight for the right to swim with the cow and calf (6). The entire group becomes very noisy and the whales swim along at great speed.

The humpback whale song is a true song like that of birds. It consists of repeated phrases, which build into a song that can be sung for many hours. All the whales in a population sing the same song, although during the season, the song gradually changes. There is a humpback whale "Top 40."

Gradually, the bulls lose interest and they peel away (7). They each return to their singing stations and start to sing. Eventually, the original bull escort leaves (8) and the cow and calf resume a more leisurely pace, swimming on alone.

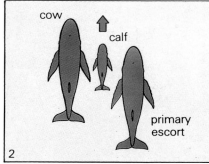

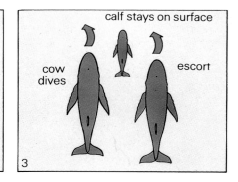

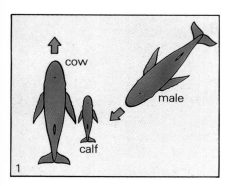

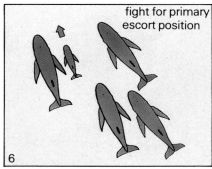

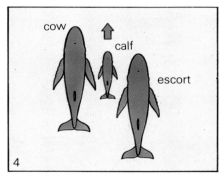

cow
calf
escort

4

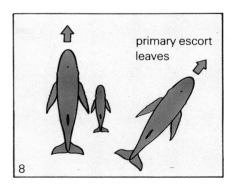

primary escort
leaves

8

Mating

It is not yet clear how female humpbacks choose their mate. Is the song more important than the ability to fight? Even more mysterious is mating. It is thought they couple with their ventral surfaces together.

Whalers tell of pairs of humpbacks that leap from the sea, separate, and then crash back into the water. Others describe whales swimming together at the surface, turning on their sides, and bringing their ventral surfaces together, the male making several passes before mating occurs.

Birth

The warm waters of the breeding grounds are ideal for giving birth. The gestation period is about a year. Nobody has seen a humpback birth, but if it is similar to a dolphin birth, then it is likely the calf is born tail first. It is born with its eyes open and can swim from the moment of birth. It will spend at least its first year accompanying its mother to and from the feeding grounds. As the calf's lungs contain no air, it has a tendency to sink, and must be nudged to the surface by the mother in order to breathe.

Index

Photographic Credits:
Cover and pages 9, 10 both, 11, 15 and 29: Bruce Coleman Ltd; pages 4-5, 21, 22, 26 and 27: Ardea; pages 6, 14, 20, 25, 28 and 31: Planet Earth; page 8 top and bottom: Mary Evans Picture Library; page 8 middle: Kendall Museum; page 12: Rex Features; page 13: Oxford Scientific Films; page 16: International Whaling Commission; pages 17 and 18: Greenpeace; page 19: Dave Curry.